psyched for science

Super Science Projects About

Energy and Motion

Allan B. Cobb

the rosen publishing group's
rosen central
new york

To my mom and dad for always encouraging my love of science and nature.

Published in 2000 by The Rosen Publishing Group, Inc.
29 East 21st Street, New York, NY 10010

First Edition

Library of Congress Cataloging-in-Publication Data

Cobb, Allan B.
    Energy and motion/ Alan B. Cobb.
      p. cm.— (Psyched for science)
    Includes bibliographical references and index.
    Summary: This book presents activities that cover five of the concepts needed to under stand energy and motion: the force of gravity, force needed to move an object, potential and kinetic energy, speed and acceleration, and work.
    ISBN 0-8239-3116-1
    1. Force and energy— Experiments— Juvenile literature. 2. Motion— Experiments— Juvenile literature. 3. Science projects— Juvenile literature. [1. Force and energy— Experiments 2. Motion— Experiments 3. Experiments 4. Science projects] I. Title.
II. Series.
    531'.078-dc21

Manufactured in the United States of America

contents

introduction

To make a car go, you give it gas. In other words, to put it in motion, you give it energy! Although this is true, there is much more to the physics of energy and motion than that.

An entire branch of physics deals with explaining energy and how it affects motion. The energy applied to an object can be measured and calculated using formulas that range from being very simple to extremely complex. The effect of energy on the motion of an object can also be measured and calculated.

In this book, the basic concepts of energy and motion will be explored with a minimum of math. The activities in this book cover five of the concepts needed to understand energy and motion: the force of gravity, the force needed to move an object, potential and kinetic energy, speed and acceleration, and work.

● **Force of gravity:** The force of gravity is important because it affects the motion of all objects. You will explore how gravity affects falling objects, and you will see how the mass of an object determines how fast it falls.

- **Force needed to move an object:** To make an object move, a force must be applied to that object. You will have an opportunity to investigate how different forces make objects move and what other forces act to keep objects from moving.

- **Potential and kinetic energy:** All objects, whether they are moving or not, have kinetic and potential energies associated with them. You will explore potential and kinetic energy as well as the transfer of energy from one body to another.

- **Speed and acceleration:** When an object is in motion, its motion can be described by its speed. When a force is applied to a moving object, this changes its speed. The measure of the change is called acceleration. You will have the opportunity to examine how speed and acceleration are measured in moving objects.

- **Work:** You will learn about how energy and work are related. In three activities, you will explore the concepts of energy, power, and chemical energy.

Spring Scale

The experiments in this book provide detailed instructions for getting started. Beyond that, they depend on your observations. Each activity has its own instructions and safety warnings. You will need to get some special materials, too. Several of the activities call for a spring scale. Spring scales are often used to weigh fish and can be found where fishing supplies are sold. You will also need a stopwatch for many of the activities; for some of them, a watch with a second hand is adequate. Many digital watches have a stopwatch function, and these are suitable for any of the timed experiments.

Digital Stop Watch

After completing these activities, you will have a better understanding of energy and motion.

1 The Pull of Gravity

Gravity is the force that causes objects to fall downward. It is a constant force and pulls all objects at the same rate. This is called the constant acceleration due to gravity.

Gravity is constantly at work. Before an airplane or bird can fly, it must overcome the pull of gravity. If you throw a ball up in the air, it must be done with enough force to overcome gravity. Once the force used to throw the ball upward becomes equal to gravity, the ball stops moving and falls back down.

The size or weight of an object has no effect on the pull of gravity. For example, an elephant and a feather experience the same gravitational pull. In this activity, you will have an opportunity to explore how the acceleration caused by gravity affects objects of different weights.

What You Need

- Two quarters

- One nickel

- A book

- A sheet of paper

The Pull of Gravity

What You'll Do

#1 Hold a quarter in each hand.

#2 Drop both quarters at the same time. Which hit the floor first?

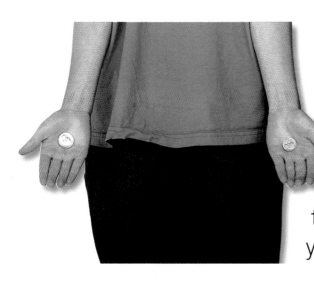

#3 If you drop a nickel and a quarter at the same time, which will hit the ground first? Hold a nickel in one hand and a quarter in the other, and then drop them at the same time. Was your prediction correct?

#4 Hold a book in one hand and a quarter in the other. If you drop them at the same time, which will hit the ground first?

#5 Drop the book and the quarter at the same time. Which hit the ground first? Was your prediction correct?

#6 Hold a book in one hand and a sheet of paper in the other hand. Which do you think will hit the ground first?

#7 Drop the book and the paper at the same time. Which hit the ground first? Was your prediction correct?

#8 Lay the sheet of paper on top of the book. If you drop them together, which will hit the ground first? Try it and find out.

The Pull of Gravity

Analyzing Your Results

#1 How accurate were your predictions about which object would hit the ground first?

#2 How did the mass of different objects affect the rates at which they fell?

#3 Why did the sheet of paper and the book fall at different rates when dropped separately but at the same rate when dropped together?

2 Constant Force and Elastic Force

As you learned in the last activity, gravity is the force that constantly pulls on objects. A related property of matter is inertia. Inertia is the tendency of a body to resist being moved or, if already moving, to resist change of direction or speed.

For a body to move or change its motion, a force must act upon it. When an object is lying on a surface, an additional force keeps it from moving: friction. Friction is the force that causes two bodies to resist motion when they are in contact with each other.

If you have ever seen a rock climber seemingly defy gravity by climbing up a wall, you have seen an example of how important friction can be. Climbers wear special shoes that provide a lot of friction against rock.

In this activity, you will explore inertia and friction and how they keep a book from moving. You will also investigate elastic forces. These are forces in which a certain amount of energy is stored and then released quickly. For example,

energy is stored in a rubber band when it is stretched and then released.

For this experiment, the best surface to use is a polished tabletop. A polished tabletop has very low friction, so the book will be easier to move.

What You Need

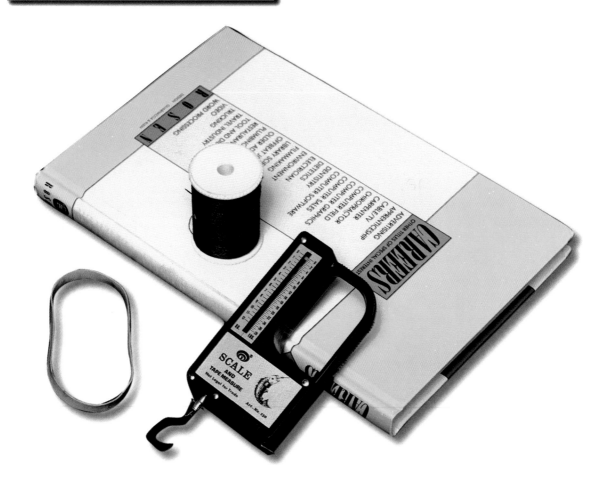

- A spring scale
- A book
- Thread
- A rubber band

Constant Force and Elastic Force

What You'll Do

#1 Open the book to approximately the middle and place a long length of thread along the spine.

#2 Close the book and tie the thread securely into a loop at one end.

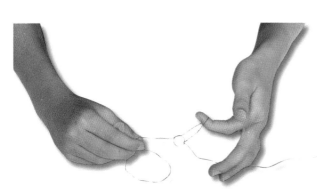

#3 Tie a small loop tightly at the other end of the thread and attach the spring scale.

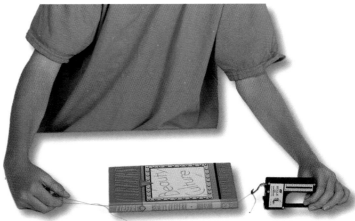

#4 Start pulling gently until the book starts to move. How much force was needed to start the book moving?

#5 Pull the book at a constant speed across a smooth surface such as a tabletop. Record the reading on the spring scale in a copy of the data table on the next page.

#6 Give the book a sharp tug. Watch the scale and record the amount of force needed to get the book moving. Note: The thread may actually break before the book moves.

#7 Attach the thread to the rubber band, and hook the spring scale to the other end of the rubber band. Start pulling gently and measure the force that is required to start the book moving.

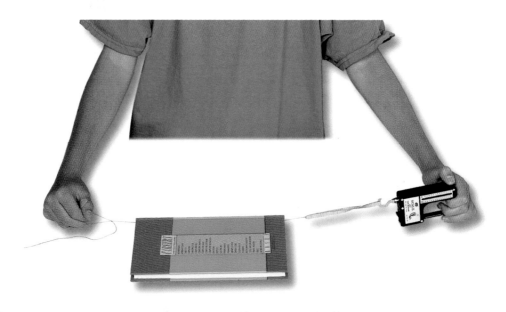

Constant Force and Elastic Force

Data Table

TYPE OF PULL	FORCE NEEDED (units)
Gentle pull	
Steady pull	
Sharp tug	
Gentle pull with rubber band	

Analyzing Your Results

#1 How did the force required to start the book moving compare to that required to keep it moving?

#2 Why do you think the rubber band made a difference in getting the book to move?

#3 What force was keeping the book from starting to move?

For Further Investigation

#1 Repeat this activity on a rough surface such as the ground. Try other surfaces such as carpet or a rug. How does the type of surface affect your results?

3 Converting Energy

Energy is the ability to do work. Physical objects may possess two different types of energy: kinetic energy and potential energy.

- Kinetic energy is the energy of motion. For example, a baseball bat hitting a baseball gives the ball kinetic energy. You can see this energy by watching the ball fly.

- Potential energy is energy that is stored because of position or configuration. A rock at the top of a cliff has potential energy. If the rock falls, it will crash down to the bottom of the cliff. A stretched rubber band also has potential energy because it is stretched. Once released, the rubber band can fly across the room.

The kinetic energy of an object depends on both its mass and its velocity. The potential energy of an object depends on its mass, its height, and the acceleration of gravity. In this activity, you will have the opportunity to explore potential and kinetic energies in objects.

What You Need

- Books
- A steel ball or large marble
- A small marble
- Two rulers (one with a groove)
- An 8-ounce paper cup
- Scissors
- Transparent tape
- Six quarters

What You'll Do

#1 Cut a 1-inch (2.5 cm) square from the top of the paper cup. The square should be large enough for the steel ball or marble to pass through easily.

#2 Set up several books on a large table or other smooth surface. Prop up the ruler with the groove to make a ramp. Place a small strip of transparent tape on the end of the ruler to secure it in place.

#3 Place the paper cup so that the ramp passes through the square cut in the cup, and the end of the ramp touches the opposite wall inside of the cup.

Converting Energy

#4 Hold the large marble at the top of the ramp and release it.

#5 Measure the distance that the paper cup moves. Record the distance in a copy of the data table on the following page.

#6 Place the paper cup in position again and place two quarters on top of it. Repeat the activity and record in the data table the distance the cup travels.

#7 Place the paper cup in position again and now place four quarters on top of it. Repeat the activity and record in the data table the distance the cup travels.

#8 Place the paper cup in position again and this time place six quarters on top of it. Repeat the activity and record in the data table the distance the cup travels.

Data Table

OBJECT	DISTANCE
Cup	
Cup and 2 quarters	
Cup and 4 quarters	
Cup and 6 quarters	

Analyzing Your Results

#1 What kind of energy did the marble have at the top of the ramp?

#2 What type of energy did the cup have sitting at the bottom of the ramp?

#3 What kind of energy did the marble have as it was rolling down the ramp?

#4 What type of energy did the cup have as it moved?

#5 How did adding quarters affect the distance that the cup traveled?

#6 Why do you think adding quarters affected the distance the cup traveled?

#7 Make a graph of your results. Put the cup and number of quarters on the x axis and the distance traveled on the y axis. Do the points make a straight line?

#8 Use your graph to determine how far the cup would move with three quarters on top. How far would the cup move with five quarters?

#9 Test your predictions by repeating the experiment with three quarters and five quarters.

#10 Do you think the graph could continue with more and more quarters added?

Experiment #3

#1 Repeat the activity with a small marble and a steel ball. How did each affect the results? Why?

4 Motion in Flight

You have heard the terms "speed" and "velocity" used interchangeably—but they do not mean the same thing. Speed is a rate, and it can be expressed in units such as miles per hour, kilometers per hour, feet per second, or centimeters per second. Velocity involves movement in a particular direction. The velocity of an object is measured by both its speed and its direction.

In this activity, you will explore the speed of a paper airplane. To find its speed, you will measure the time it takes to cover a certain distance. The speed you will find is an average, since you are looking at the speed averaged over a certain distance. (The speed from the speedometer of a car is instantaneous because it represents the speed the car is going at a particular time.)

For this activity, you will need a friend to help you time the flight of the paper airplane. This activity is best done outside in an open area with little or no wind. Be careful when throwing your airplane that it does not strike anyone or any object that is easily damaged.

Speedometer

Motion in Flight

What You Need

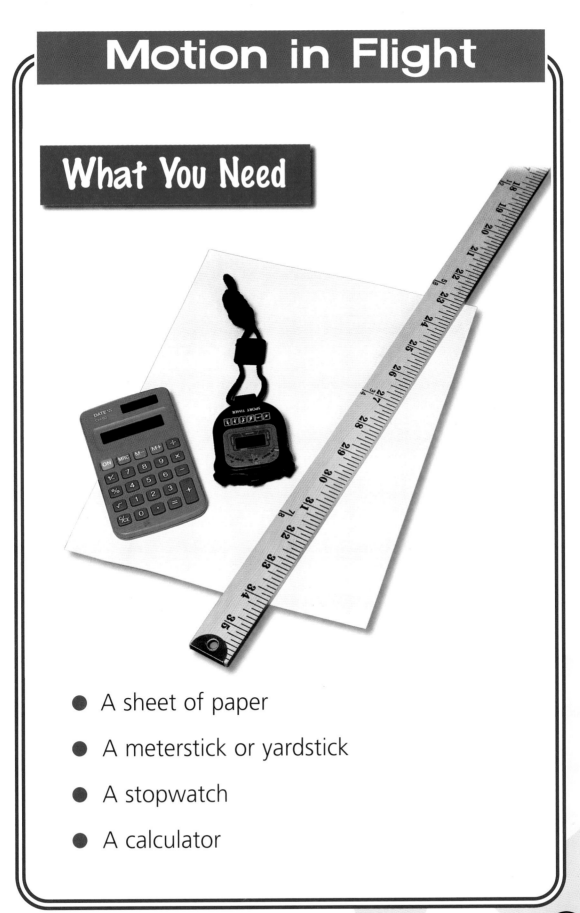

- A sheet of paper
- A meterstick or yardstick
- A stopwatch
- A calculator

27

Experiment #4

What You'll Do

#1 Fold the paper to make a paper airplane.

#2 Choose an outside location where you can measure a distance of 3 or 4 yards (or 3 or 4 meters). Mark the two ends of the distance so that they are easily visible.

#3 Stand just behind one of the distance markers and throw the paper airplane so that it travels in a straight path to the other distance marker. Have your partner time how long it takes the plane to fly between the distance markers.

Motion in Flight

#4 Repeat the timed flights until you have thrown the airplane five times. Each time you throw the plane, try to use the same amount of force.

Data Table

FLIGHT #	DISTANCE (d)	TIME (t)	SPEED(d/t)
1			
2			
3			
4			
5			

Analyzing Your Results

#1 Calculate the speed of your plane in each flight by dividing the distance by the time. Write the speed in the data table.

#2 What is the average speed of the plane? Find this by adding up all the speeds and then dividing by the number of flights.

Experiment #4

#3 How do you think the speed of the paper airplane would be affected if you used more force to throw it?

#4 Were the speeds you calculated actual or average speeds?

#5 How do you think the calculated speed of the plane would change if the measured distance was increased or decreased?

For Further Investigation

#1 Repeat the activity with different styles of paper airplanes. Do some fly faster?

#2 Repeat the activity with paper airplanes of the same style but made from different weights of paper. How does the weight of the paper affect the speed?

5 Energy and Work

"Energy" and "work" are two common terms used in physics. Energy is the capacity to do work. "Work" is a term used to describe the force applied to an object to make it move. Work is done only when a force causes a change in the motion of an object. For example, holding a book does not involve work, but lifting a book from a table does involve work. Work is calculated by multiplying the force applied to an object by the distance that the object is moved.

In this activity, a ramp is used to change the distance over which the force is applied. A ramp is a simple machine that turns a small force into a large force by spreading the work over a long distance rather than just lifting. By measuring and calculating the work involved in two different ways of moving an object, you will explore how a ramp makes work easier.

What You Need

- A brick

- A board

- A meterstick or yardstick

- Books

- A spring scale

- A roller skate

- String

Energy and Work

What You'll Do

#1 Stack up the books and lean the board against them to make a ramp. Measure the distance up the ramp as well as the height of the ramp. Record the distances in a copy of the data table on the following page.

#2 Place a brick inside the roller skate.

#3 Attach the spring scale to the roller skate and place the setup on the ramp.

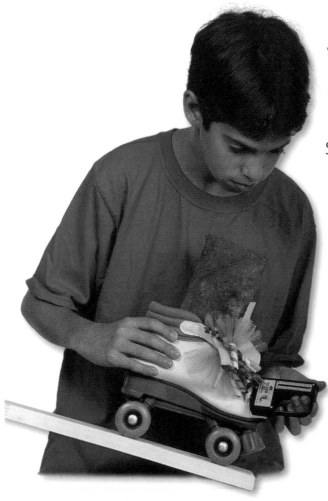

#4 Hold the spring scale parallel to the ramp and pull the roller skate up the ramp at a constant speed. Record in your data table the force necessary to pull the roller skate up the ramp.

#5 With the scale attached to the roller skate and the brick, raise them the height of the ramp and record the force required.

Data Table

Length of ramp (f1)	Force required to pull up the ramp (d1)	Height of ramp (f2)	Force required to lift up (d2)

Energy and Work

Analyzing Your Results

#1 Calculate the work required to pull the roller skate and brick up the ramp. The formula for finding the work is $w = f1 \times d1$.

#2 Calculate the work required to lift the roller skate and brick up to the height of the ramp. The formula for finding the work is $w = f2 \times d2$.

#3 How do the two amounts of work compare?

For Further Investigation

#1 Repeat the activity using different masses. How do the results compare?

#2 Repeat the activity using just a brick instead of the brick and roller skate. How do the results compare? Why is it harder to pull just the brick up the ramp than the brick with the roller skate? What could you do to make it easier to pull the brick?

6 Chemical Energy

One way that energy can be stored is in the chemical bonds of compounds. The energy stored in chemical bonds can have tremendous power.

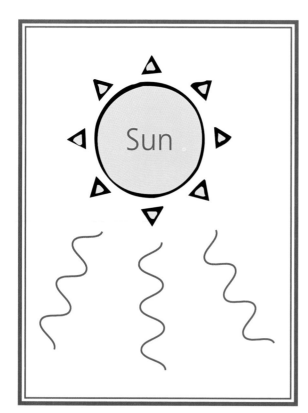

Take the sun, for example. All of the light, heat, and other energy the sun emits come from energy stored in chemical bonds.

In this activity, you will explore the energy stored in the chemical bonds in baking soda.

What You Need

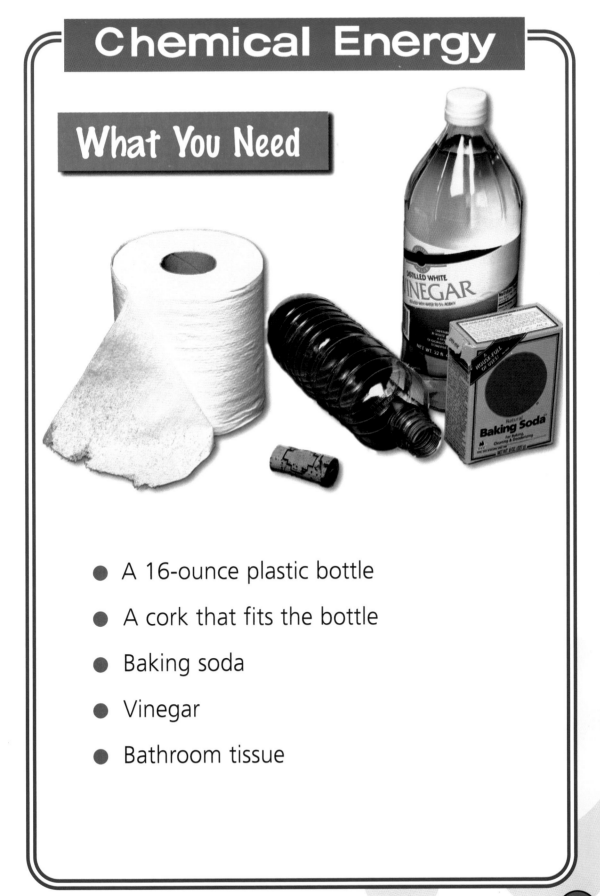

- A 16-ounce plastic bottle
- A cork that fits the bottle
- Baking soda
- Vinegar
- Bathroom tissue

What You'll Do

#1 Place about 1 teaspoon of baking soda on the bathroom tissue and fold it into a packet small enough to fit inside the neck of the plastic bottle.

#2 Pour approximately 3 ounces of vinegar into the bottle.

#3 Put the small packet containing the baking soda into the bottle and quickly cork the bottle. Make sure that the bottle is not pointing toward anyone, and stand back from it.

#4 Observe what happens to the cork.

Experiment #6

Analyzing Your Results

#1 Why do you think the cork popped out of the bottle?

#2 Where did the force that caused the cork to pop out of the bottle come from?

#3 How could you measure the energy produced?

For Further Investigation

Repeat the activity with varying amounts of vinegar and baking soda. How does this affect the height to which the cork shoots or the amount of time it takes the cork to shoot from the bottle?

glossary

acceleration   The rate of change in velocity.

chemical bonds   The attractive force by which atoms are held together.

chemical energy   Energy stored in chemical bonds.

elastic force   Force stored in a temporary change in shape, such as stretching or compressing.

energy   The ability to do work.

force   Anything that affects a body at rest or in motion.

gravity   The natural force that attracts objects.

inertia   The resistance of a body at rest to motion.

kinetic energy   The energy of motion.

potential energy   Energy stored in an object because of its location or configuration.

power   The rate of doing work.

speed   The rate at which something moves.

velocity   The speed of an object in a particular direction.

work   Force applied to an object to set it in motion.

reSOurces

These Web sites will help you find out more about energy and motion:

Cool Science for Curious Kids
http://www.hhmi.org/coolscience

Cyberspace Middle School—Science Fair Projects
http://www.scri.fsu.edu/~dennisl/special/sf_projects.
   html

Exploratorium
http://www.exploratorium.edu

The Franklin Institute
http://sln.fi.edu

Mad Scientist Network
http://www.madsci.org

National Science Foundation Science in the Home
http://www.ehr.nsf.gov/ehr/ehr/science_home/html/
   about.htm

The Science Club
http://www.halcyon.com/sciclub

resources

Science Fair Project Ideas
http://othello.mech.nwu.edu/~peshkin/scifair/index.html

Scientific American Explore!
http://www.sciam.com/explorations

Smithsonian Institute
http://www.si.edu

for further reading

Challoner, Jack. *Eyewitness Science: Energy.* New York: DK Publishing, 1993.

DiSpezio, Michael Anthony. *Awesome Experiments in Force & Motion.* New York: Sterling Publications, 1998.

Doherty, Paul. *The Cool Hot Rod and Other Electrifying Experiments on Energy and Matter (The Exploratorium Science Snackbook Series).* New York: John Wiley & Sons, 1996.

Doherty, Paul. *The Spinning Blackboard and Other Dynamic Experiments on Force and Motion (Exploratorium Science Snackbook Series).* New York: John Wiley & Sons, 1996.

Franklin, Sharon. *Power Up! Energy (Explore Science).* New York: Goodyear Publications Company, 1995.

Morgan, Sally. *Using Energy (Designs in Science).* New York: Facts on File, Inc., 1994.

for further reading

Snedden, Robert. *Energy (Science Horizons).* New York: Chelsea House Publishers, 1995.

Spurgeon, Robert. *Energy and Power (Science and Experiments).* New York: E D C Publications, 1990.

index

index

credits

About the Author

Allan Cobb is a freelance science writer living in Central Texas. He has written books, radio scripts, articles, and educational material concerning different aspects of science. When not writing about science, he enjoys traveling, camping, hiking, and exploring caves.

Photo Credits

Cover photos by Scott Bauer. P. 7 © Skjold Photographs; p. 13 © Poulet/Wallis/Photri Inc. All other photos by Scott Bauer.

Design and Layout

Laura Murawski

Consulting Editor

Amy Haugesag

Metric Conversions

To convert measurements in U.S. units into metric units, use the following formulas:

1 inch = 2.54 centimeters (cm)	1 ounce = 28.35 grams (g)
1 foot = 0.30 meters (m)	1 gallon = 3.79 liters (l)
1 mile = 1.609 kilometers (km)	1 pound = 453.59 grams (g)